The Story of
Writing

Carol Donoughue

FIREFLY BOOKS

*For David, my children, their partners,
and my grandchildren.*

A FIREFLY BOOK

Published by Firefly Books Ltd. 2007

First printing

Publisher Cataloging-in-Publication Data (U.S.)

Donoughue, Carol.
    The story of writing / Carol Donoughue.
[48] p. : col. illl. ; cm.
Includes bibliographical references and index.
Summary: The story of the invention of writing and how it developed over the centuries as peoples lives and the need to communicate changed.
ISBN-13: 978-1-55407-306-1
ISBN-10: 1-55407-306-5
1. Writing—History—Juvenile literature. I. Title.
411.09 dc22   P211.D69   2007

Library and Archives Canada Cataloguing in Publication

Donoughue, Carol
    The story of writing / Carol Donoughue.
Includes bibliographical references and index.
ISBN-13: 978-1-55407-306-1
ISBN-10: 1-55407-306-5
    1. Writing—History—Juvenile literature. I. Title.
P211.D69 2007   j411'.09   C2007-901504-2

Published in the United States by
Firefly Books (U.S.) Inc.
P.O. Box 1338, Ellicott Station
Buffalo, New York 14205

Published in Canada by
Firefly Books Ltd.
66 Leek Crescent
Richmond Hill, Ontario L4B 1H1

Designed and typeset by Peter Bailey for Proof Books
Printed and bound in Singapore.

AUTHOR'S ACKNOWLEDGEMENTS

This book would not have been written without the generous help and advice of the curators in the Departments of Ancient Egypt and Sudan, Greece and Rome, Prehistory and Europe, Middle East, and Asia at the British Museum.

I would also like to thank Justin Clegg, John Goldfinch and Alan Sterenberg at the British Library for their guidance. The Camden Professor of Ancient History at Oxford University, Alan Bowman, the librarian and Curator at Winchester Cathedral, John Hardacre, Gabriel Goldstein HMI and Sun Shuyun, author and broadcaster, have all spent much time and effort on my behalf. Normand Park Primary School in London kindly gave me copies of their school newspaper.

Carolyn Jones, my editor, Beatriz Waters, the picture editor, and Peter Bailey, the designer have worked long hours without complaint. All my thanks to them.

ILLUSTRATION ACKNOWLEDGEMENTS

Unless otherwise stated, photographs are © The Trustees of the British Museum, taken by the British Museum Dept of Photography and Imaging.

The publishers have made every effort to contact the copyright-holders of all illustrations, but if notified in writing of any errors or omissions will be happy to make corrections at the next reprint.

Victor Ambrus p. 22 bottom.
Prof Alan Bowman p. 22 top.
Bridgeman Art Library/Louvre, Paris/Lauros/Giraudon p.17 top right;
Bridgeman Art Library/Victoria & Albert Museum, London p. 30 left.
Bristol Record Office p. 30 right.
British Library: p. 2, p. 27 top left, p. 31 top left, top right and bottom right, p. 32 top, p. 34 left and bottom right, p. 35 top.
Corbis: p. 44 top left; Corbis/© Jose Luis Pelaez, Inc.: p. 4 top right; Corbis/Rob Lewine: p. 44 top right; Corbis/Roger Wood: p. 11 top right.
Mike Corbishley: p. 26 bottom right.
The Dean and Chapter of Winchester, photo © John Hardacre: p. 29 bottom.
DK Images p. 33 top, p. 34 top right.
Irving Finkel p. 6 top, p. 7 top and bottom left, p. 9.
Quotation from Khalil Gibran, *The Mad Man: His parables and poems* (Arab Publishing House): p. 21 top left.
Patricia Hansom p. 6 bottom right, p.19, p. 20 centre right, p. 24 bottom left, p. 25 top left; p. 31 bottom left.
Graham Harrison p. 14 top.
Louvre © RMN - Jérôme Galland: p. 8 bottom left.
ML Design: p. 47 map.
Richard Parkinson: p. 12 top, p. 13 top right, p. 15 centre.
Qu Lei Lei, *Chinese Calligraphy* (BMP 2004): p. 40 top.
Dr. Ludwig Reichert Verlag, Wiesbaden: p. 1, p. 4 top left, p. 27 bottom right.
The Royal Library, Copenhagen. The Manuscripts Dept.: p. 28, p. 29 top.
Sun Shuyun: Chinese characters p. 40 bottom, p. 41, p. 42.
Claire Thorne: p. 16 bottom.
© Photo Scala, Florence/Naples Museum Nazionale 2003: p. 26 top left.
Science & Society Picture Library/National Museum of Photography, Film and Television: p. 39 top left; Science & Society Picture Library/Science Museum p. 39 top right, centre and bottom right.
Staatliche Museen zu Berlin-Preussischer Kulturbesitz Antikensammlung. Photo Johannes Laurentius: p. 21 bottom right.
V & A Picture Library: p. 36, p. 37, p.38 left, p. 38 centre right and bottom right, p. 39 bottom left.

Contents

Why writing?

Two medieval monks writing in a scriptorium.

What have you written today? Have you written something in school – a story, or notes on something you have read, or a description of a science experiment? Have you written something at home – a diary or a letter or a text or email message to a friend? Did you use a computer, or did you write on paper with a pen?

By writing things down we can store information, we can communicate with other people and we can remind ourselves of things we have done or things we need to do. If we couldn't write things down, we would have to rely on talking and listening – and having a very good memory.

This book tells the story of how different people in different parts of the world invented their own ways of writing things down. It is about how writing came to be invented hundreds of years ago because people needed to remember things and to send messages.

These clay tablets may be more than 5,000 years old. The signs on them mean '10 goats' and '10 sheep'.

In the British Museum, and in other museums, you can look at writing from all periods of history and all parts of the world.

PICTOGRAMS

The story begins about 6,000 years ago. Rulers and important people wanted to keep records to make sure things weren't forgotten. Without writing, how could they do it? At first, people drew pictures to stand for objects. We call those pictures **pictograms**.

We still use pictures today to give information. We sometimes call these pictures 'icons'.

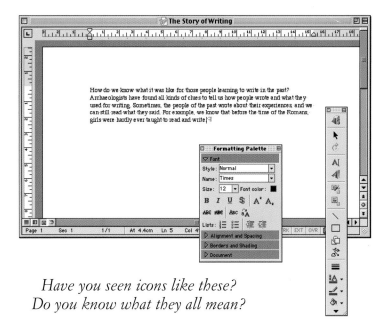

We use icons in this book. In every chapter except Chapter 3 there is a sign like this and the words 'You are …' When you see this icon you can travel back through time and imagine that you are learning to write at a certain time and place.

Have you seen icons like these?
Do you know what they all mean?

Chapter 3 describes the invention of our alphabet (a b c d e f g h i j k l m n o p q r s t u v w x y z). So far, **archaeologists** have not found anything from that period that tells us how children learned to write. So, you will not find the icon in that chapter.

CLUES FROM THE PAST

How do we know what it was like for those people learning to write in the past? Archaeologists have found all kinds of clues to tell us how people wrote and what they used for writing. Sometimes, the people of the past described how they learned to write and we can still read their words. For example, we know that before Roman times, girls were hardly ever taught to read and write.

Two Egyptian scribes.

At the beginning of each chapter you will find words that people in history have written about writing. You will see how much writing varies in different places at different times.

FIND OUT MORE

On some pages of the book you will find an icon like this and the words 'Find out more'. Under this icon there is more information about writing at that time in history and about the people of the period. There is also a map on page 47 to help you work out where the different kinds of writing in this book come from.

You will see that some words are printed in **bold print**. That means you will find an explanation of what they mean in the Glossary on page 46.

The Sumerians and cuneiform

'A scribe who does not know Sumerian, what kind of scribe is he?'

This writing is called cuneiform. It was invented by the Sumerians in Mesopotamia some time before 3000 BC. The different peoples of Mesopotamia used cuneiform writing for thousands of years. These words come from a collection of proverbs, or sayings, written about 1700 BC, which had to be copied by young boys learning to become scribes.

You are ...

... a young Sumerian boy learning how to write. Your teacher has drawn some signs like this

Teacher's writing   *Boy's copies*

on a flat piece of soft clay and he has told you to copy them on to the other side of the tablet. He's shown you how to cut a piece of reed to make a **stylus**.

By pressing the straight edge of the stylus into the clay you can make vertical and horizontal wedges. If you press the corner of the stylus into the clay you can make the little arrowhead mark.

Making cuneiform signs with a stylus.

There are more than 600 cuneiform signs, but all of them are made from a combination of these three marks.

vertical *horizontal* *diagonal*

You've already spent weeks and weeks learning to make the wedge-shaped marks clearly and cleanly with your stylus. One of the older boys helped you with that. Now you're getting better and the teacher has decided you can start to copy some signs and words. It isn't easy. You'd better try again because the teacher might come and beat you if you don't get it right soon. One of your friends sitting over there in the corner has already had a beating and he's still sniffling over his clay tablet. If you take too long the clay will start to harden and you won't be able to rub out your mistakes with the stylus.

You are learning how to write so that you can become a **scribe**. Not many people can write and read – not even the king. The only people who learn to write are the priests, doctors and some of the merchants. So when you have learned to write, you will be needed by everybody who wants something written down. All this hard work and the beatings will be worth it!

Cow

The teacher has given you easy signs to copy, such as this one, which stands for 'cow'.

Ox

They can get much more complicated, like this one which stands for 'ox'.

The teacher has a sign list that is used by all the scribes so that they use the same signs and they know what each sign means.

Ox

Your father works as a scribe. He told you that hundreds of years ago the ox picture, and all the other signs, used to be written standing upright like this. It looked much more like an ox.

Two Assyrian scribes writing, one on a wax tablet and the other on a parchment scroll.

Soon it will be time to go home. You can leave your tablet with the teacher. He will put it where the sun will bake it hard. Tomorrow he will make another tablet from the clay along the riverbank for you to use.

The earliest kind of writing to be discovered by **archaeologists** comes from Mesopotamia, the area between the Tigris and Euphrates rivers that today is Iraq. There was a country in Mesopotamia called Sumer. At the site of a great temple there, clay tablets written in about 3000 BC were found, covered in mysterious signs.

The oldest clay objects found were clay shapes that stood for animals, food, oil or garments.

These clay shapes stand for different things, including sheep, honey and oil.

This was probably the way that farmers recorded what goods they had traded with another farmer. Later, people started to use flat clay tablets with marks written on them. They didn't bother with the shapes of the animals. The writing was enough to remind them of what they had traded.

These marks stand for 'ten goats' and 'ten sheep'.

The Sumerians wrote other kinds of information on clay tablets, too. This one records how many workmen were working at a temple – 18 bakers, 31 brewers, 7 slaves and 1 blacksmith.

PICTURE SIGNS

At first, scribes used **pictograms** – signs that looked like objects. This was the first sign for a fish, from about 3000 BC:

The **scribes** soon found that they could make neater, clearer writing if they pressed the edge or corner of a flat **stylus** into the clay instead of trying to pull a pointed stylus across the surface. So they began to write with straight lines instead of curved shapes. The sign for a fish started to look like this:

Some of the signs had more than one meaning. For example, the sign for 'foot' could also mean 'to walk' or 'to move'.

SOUND SIGNS

Another change happened gradually over many years. Scribes began to use some of the signs to stand for the sounds of the Sumerian language and not just for pictures of objects. In other words, those signs were not pictograms but **phonograms** (sound signs). The scribes were using a sign not for what it looked like but for what it sounded like.

For example, the word 'arrow' sounded like 'ti' in Sumerian. The same 'arrow' sign was also used for the word 'life', which also sounded like 'ti'. It would be difficult to make a pictogram for the word 'life'. What would you draw?

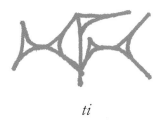

ti

SYLLABLES

In cuneiform writing each sign stands for a **syllable**, a sound such as 'ti', 'gu' or 'ud'.

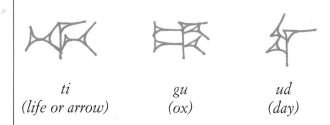

ti	*gu*	*ud*
(life or arrow)	*(ox)*	*(day)*

This is very different from the alphabet we use, which has a letter for every single **consonant** and **vowel** sound.

Sumerian 'inscriptions' (pieces of writing) in cuneiform have been found on thousands of clay tablets and sometimes on statues and sculptures. Some of them are to do with buying and selling, some of them are marriage contracts or wills or lists of goods for sale. The documents were often put into envelopes made of clay. Sometimes the document was then written again on the envelope. That way, if the outside envelope was defaced, people could open it and find another, undamaged, copy of the writing inside.

DECIPHERING CUNEIFORM

Cuneiform writing was used for around 3,000 years to write the languages of all the peoples of Mesopotamia: the Sumerians, the Assyrians and the Babylonians. The latest cuneiform inscription was written in AD 75. After that, cuneiform died out and its secrets were lost. More than 1,600 years went by before anyone could understand cuneiform once more.

From the 18th century AD onwards, **scholars** tried to **decipher** this writing. They gave it the name 'cuneiform', from the Latin word *cuneus* meaning 'wedge-shaped', because the signs are made up of wedges. The great breakthrough was made by a British army officer called Sir Henry

This boundary stone shows a king with a carved inscription (at his knee).

Sir Henry Rawlinson.

Rawlinson in the 1840s. He found a gigantic inscription carved in three languages on a cliff near the town of Bisitun in modern Iran. Swinging precariously from ropes, Rawlinson made a copy of the whole inscription. First he deciphered the Old Persian, and then he deciphered the Babylonian. Cuneiform could be read once more.

The cliff inscription near Bisitun.

LEGENDS AND STORIES

Not all the clay tablets are business or legal documents. There are also stories and poems. The most famous story is 'The Epic of Gilgamesh'. It is about a king who is part human and part god. With his friend Enkidu he has many adventures, kills monsters, and seeks the secret of eternal life. This copy of the story was written down about 700 BC, though the story itself is much older. In this passage Gilgamesh kills a terrible giant called Humbaba, who guards a cedar forest.

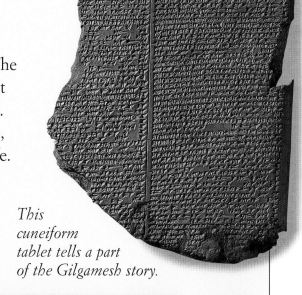

This cuneiform tablet tells a part of the Gilgamesh story.

'Gilgamesh struck Humbaba in the neck. His friend Enkidu shouted at him to do it again. Humbaba sank down and the hillside ran with his blood. Gilgamesh struck Humbaba to the ground. He killed the ogre who guarded the forest. Humbaba's yells made the mountains shake and the hillsides tremble. The peaks of Sirion and Lebanon were split apart by the dreadful noise.'

A seal and its impression, showing Gilgamesh and Enkidu fighting Humbaba.

2 The Egyptians and hieroglyphs

'Then he stretched his hand out to a box of writing equipment.
Then he took for himself a roll and a palette.
And he was writing down
What the lector-priest Neferti said.'

These signs are hieroglyphs. Ancient Egyptian priests wrote in hieroglyphs. They called the hieroglyphic script 'the writing of the divine words' because they used it to write about their gods and their pharaohs.

You are ...

... kneeling on the ground with a group of boys. You are all listening hard to your teacher who is reading out some words from the long roll of papyrus he is holding in front of him. Usually you copy from other papyrus rolls, but today he is giving you a test. On the ground beside you on your left is the end of your papyrus roll and in your right hand you are holding a reed pen. You are trying to write down the words that the teacher is saying. You wish he wouldn't go so fast, because now and again you have to rub the brush end of your pen over a block of black colour in the palette beside you. You also have to unwind

Two scribes writing.

A scribe's palette, inks and brushes.

the papyrus roll with your left hand after you've filled up all the empty space with signs. Then you must put your pen down on the ground and roll up what you've written with your right hand.

You usually begin your lines of signs on the right and write towards the left. There are hundreds and hundreds of signs and you have to remember how to write them all. When you started school you had to practise writing them on bits of broken pottery called ostraca. You've only just been allowed to write on papyrus all the time.

Unrolling a papyrus.

Will you be able to remember everything? If you make too many mistakes the teacher will get angry and beat you. The old **scribes** say, 'A boy's ears are on his back; he listens when he is beaten'.

The teacher has already made you all stand up and repeat after him over and over again a long list of the names of the pharaohs. And now here you are, with the papyrus roll on your knees, trying to concentrate. Oh! He's just said a word that you don't understand. It must be one of those foreign words. How are you going to write that one? You've probably made a mistake, but he's not giving you any time to think about it.

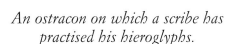

An ostracon on which a scribe has practised his hieroglyphs.

Can you see the teacher's corrections written at the top of this papyrus?

Wall carving of the pharaoh Ramesses II from his temple at Abu Simbel.

If you learn all those signs and you do well, then, the teacher says, you can start to learn how to write the signs that are written on the walls of the temples. That's much more interesting than just writing on papyrus. It means that, when you are older, you might get work in the temple that the pharaoh is building on the banks of the Nile, writing the story of a battle that he has just won. That would be better than just making lists of sacks of grain at harvest time, or how many geese a farmer has, or even writing about medicines and how to cure illnesses. But it will mean learning even more, different signs, and ones that are harder to write ... You'd better concentrate on the test! Now your pen is wearing out. The reed has bent because you've been holding it too tight and the brush end is making a mess on the papyrus ... When will he stop? Now he's stopped. You can get up and stretch your legs!

This scribe is writing down how many geese a farmer has, and working out how much tax the farmer will pay.

The hieroglyphic **script** appeared in ancient Egypt by about 3100 BC. Some experts think that the Egyptians were influenced by Sumerian cuneiform, but others believe that the Egyptians invented writing quite independently.

Like the Sumerians, the Egyptian **scribes** began by using **pictograms**, but then they started to use **phonograms** (sound signs)

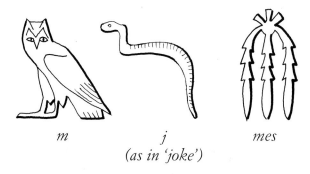

| m | j | mes |
| | *(as in 'joke')* | |

and also **ideograms** – signs that stand for ideas or things.

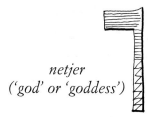

| netjer | re |
| *('god' or 'goddess')* | *('sun' or 'day')* |

They did not leave spaces between the words so that thewritinglookedlikethis. They sometimes wrote from left to right, but often they wrote from right to left or from top to bottom.

The hieroglyphs on this coffin are written from top to bottom and from side to side.

Sometimes the scribe just fitted the hieroglyphs around the picture he was describing.

A wall painting from the tomb chapel of a man called Nebamun.

There were no commas and no full stops.

They also used special signs that we call **determinatives** to tell the reader what kind of word was being written.

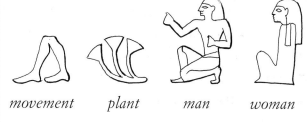

| movement | plant | man | woman |

THREE KINDS OF WRITING

Hieroglyphs always remained the most important kind of writing in ancient Egypt but they were not the only Egyptian script. Egyptian scribes developed two other ways of writing. The boys you read about on pages 12–13 were learning how to write the **hieratic** script, which was a simplified version of hieroglyphs. It was used mainly by priests to write on papyrus.

This papyrus was written in hieratic script in about 1200 BC. It describes how to tell the meaning of dreams.

DECIPHERING HIEROGLYPHS

For centuries, scholars tried to work out what hieroglyphs meant. They travelled to Egypt and saw beautiful temples, monuments and pyramids covered with writing. They knew that if only they could understand the hieroglyphs they would know all about how the Egyptians lived, but it was too difficult. After the 7th century AD, the Egyptians no longer spoke the same language as they had before. Even they could not help to solve the mystery.

There was also a third **script** which we call **demotic**. This was used for informal, everyday writing. Only the priests and the scribes and their apprentices could write or understand the different kinds of writing. Most people in ancient Egypt could not read or write at all.

Then in 1799 a French soldier in Napoleon's army fighting against the English in Egypt discovered, at a place called Rosetta, a large stone covered with three different kinds of writing. One of them was Greek. The soldier realized that

PAPYRUS

Papyrus is the name of a reed used by the ancient Egyptians for making a kind of paper. They cut the stem into thin slices and laid some lengthways and others across them. Then they moistened the layers with water, pressed them with a heavy weight and dried them. When the layers were dry, they stuck together to form a sheet. The sheet was rubbed smooth and then it was ready to be used to write on. The sheets were joined together into rolls, some of which were very long indeed – several metres (yards) long.

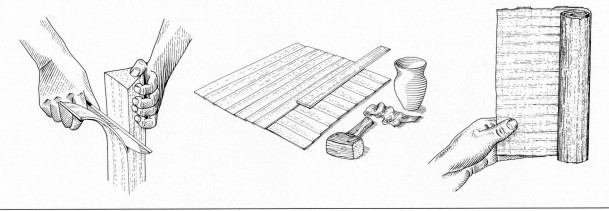

another part of the stone was written in hieroglyphs. Did the hieroglyphs say the same thing as the Greek writing? Most scholars could understand Greek, so it might be possible to work out what the hieroglyphs said. The soldier decided that it was an important find and he took it back to his general. But the French lost the battle with the English and the English general took the Rosetta Stone back to England. Today you can see it in the British Museum.

The Rosetta Stone

hieroglyphs

Demotic

Greek

Copies of the writing on the Rosetta Stone were sent to scholars all over Europe so that they could try to work out what the writing meant. In France, a young man called Jean François Champollion spent fifteen years trying to decipher the hieroglyphs. Even though he could read the Greek writing, he could not manage to solve the mystery. Then one day, in 1822, he finally made a breakthrough. He understood that many of the signs stood

Jean François Champollion.

for the *sounds* of the ancient Egyptian language. He was able to decipher all the hieroglyphs. Now it was possible to read all that the ancient Egyptians had written about themselves.

AN ANCIENT EGYPTIAN MATHEMATICAL PROBLEM

Fat worth 10 gallons is issued for one year. What is the daily share of it? The working out: you shall make this fat worth 10 gallons into *ro**; this makes 3,200. You shall make the year into days; this makes 365. You shall divide 3,200 by 365; this makes $8 + 2/3 + 1/10 + 1/2,190$ ($= 8.767$) … This is the daily share.

* *ro* = an Egyptian measurement; there were 3,200 ro to the gallon.

3 The first alphabet

A B C D E F G H I J K L M N O P Q R S T U V W X Y Z

This is the alphabet we use today in most countries in the West.

The invention of the alphabet was one of the most important and far-reaching events in the whole history of writing, but *exactly* how, when and where it happened remains a mystery.

WHAT IS AN ALPHABET?

An alphabet is a writing system that has a single letter for each **consonant** and **vowel** sound. In effect, it's a toolbox from which a writer can choose whatever he or she needs to write down the sounds of any language.

An alphabet is much easier to learn than other writing systems, so it should make it possible for more people to learn to read and write. A **scribe** writing in hieroglyphs or cuneiform had to learn hundreds and hundreds of different signs. A person writing in our modern Western alphabet has to learn only twenty-six letters.

THE BEGINNING OF THE ALPHABET

How did the alphabet start? Did it develop out of the older writing systems, cuneiform and hieroglyphs? Did one person have a brilliant brainwave one day and just invent an alphabet? Nobody really knows. We have got tantalizing evidence that people tried alphabetic writing more than once before the alphabet we know was finally established.

Archaeologists have found more than 1,000 tablets written in the Ugaritic cuneiform alphabet – business and legal documents, poems, stories and spells.

The oldest alphabetic writing we know about appeared in Ugarit (northern Syria) in about 1400 BC. Someone in Ugarit had the clever idea of making up thirty easy-to-learn cuneiform signs to stand for the sounds that they needed to write their language.

There are even school tablets with lists of signs for schoolboys to copy when they were learning to write the 'cuneiform alphabet'.

The Ugaritic 'cuneiform alphabet' died out about 1200 BC, but after about 200 years another alphabet appeared in Phoenicia. It had twenty-two letters – almost all consonants.

Nobody knows exactly why or how this new alphabet developed. It was probably a mixture, using some ideas from Egyptian hieroglyphs and some ideas from other **scripts**. Look carefully and compare it with the Ugaritic cuneiform alphabet. The letter shapes are quite different, and there are fewer letters, but the order of the sounds is almost identical, even though the Ugaritic writing had disappeared 200 years before ...

LEFT The Ugaritic 'cuneiform alphabet'. It has thirty letters to write all the sounds of the Ugaritic language.

The Ugaritic signs (left column): ʼa, b, g, ḫ, d, h, w, z, ḥ, ṭ, y, k, š, l, m — and (right column): ḏ, n, ẓ, s, ʼ, p, ṣ, q, r, ṯ, ġ, t, i, ʼu, ṡ

BELOW The Phoenician alphabet, 200 years later.

a	b	g	d	h	w	z	h	t	y	k	l	m	r	s	ʼ	p	s	q	r	s	t

THE SPREAD OF THE ALPHABET

Phoenician traders, who lived along the coast of the Mediterranean Sea (see the map on page 47) sailed to other countries to buy and sell their goods and they took their alphabet with them.

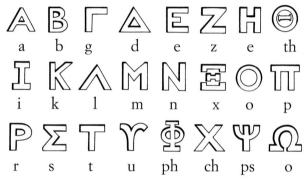

A stone carving of a Phoenician galley.

In that way, the new alphabet spread around the shores of the Mediterranean. It was much easier to use than any of the earlier writing systems. The Ancient Greeks, with whom the Phoenicians traded, began to copy it.

The ancient Greeks started to add vowels to the new alphabet. Their language needed to have vowel sounds written down because it would have been confusing without them. (Imagine writing 'nt' and hoping that people would understand you meant 'not'. Your readers would have to work out if you meant 'not' – or 'net', or 'auntie', or 'untie', or 'unite' ...) Adding vowels makes it much clearer. The ancient Greek alphabet had twenty-four letters. It looked like this:

A	B	Γ	Δ	E	Z	H	Θ
a	b	g	d	e	z	e	th

I	K	Λ	M	N	Ξ	O	Π
i	k	l	m	n	x	o	p

P	Σ	T	Υ	Φ	X	Ψ	Ω
r	s	t	u	ph	ch	ps	o

The ancient Greek alphabet.

LINEAR B

This was not the first time that the ancient Greek language had been written down.

Two Linear B tablets. The small tablet records the number of sheep in a place called Phaistos and the large one describes offering oil to the gods.

These tablets were written in the thirteenth century BC. They were discovered in the Palace of Knossos on Crete by the **archaeologist** Arthur Evans. He could not **decipher** them. He called the script Linear B. It wasn't until 1952 that Michael Ventris managed to break the code, recognizing that the language was Greek. This writing system is not an alphabet. Some signs stand for **syllables** and some are **logograms**. This writing died out, but it may have had an influence on the new alphabet.

A Greek inscription. On the first line the letters run from left to right. On the second line they run from right to left, and so on. We call this change of direction boustrophedon, *a Greek word meaning 'as the ox ploughs'.*

A Greek athlete painted on a pot, with his name written beside him.

Greek writing did not have any commas or full stops in it. There were no gaps between words soitlookedlikethis. So it can be difficult for us to read it today. In the earliest Greek inscriptions the **scribe** wrote from left to right on one line and then from right to left on the next.

By about 600 BC, the Greeks seem to have decided that all the lines should run from left to right, like our writing today. (Do you know of any other kinds of writing that run from right to left?)

A Greek boy learning to read and write. The boy and his teacher are painted on a cup.

4 The Romans and writing

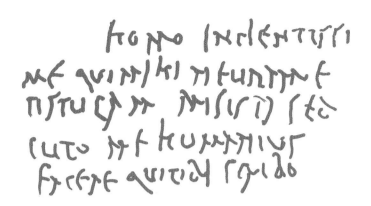

'You neglectful man who have sent me not even one letter. I think I am behaving in a more considerate fashion in writing to you.'

A Roman called Sollemnis wrote this letter to his friend Paris in the 1st century AD. Paris was probably the slave of a Roman army commander serving in northern Britain. The letter shows that by that time many Romans, as well as the people in the countries they conquered, knew how to write and regularly sent each other letters.

You are ...

... a young woman called Claudia Severa and you live with your husband, Aelius Brocchus, and your little son in a fort in the north of England. Your husband is an officer in the Roman army. Your birthday is in the middle of September and you want to invite your best friend, Sulpicia Lepidina, to your birthday party. She lives in Vindolanda, which is another fort not very far away. She is the wife of Flavius Cerialis, who leads the 9th cohort of Batavian soldiers.

You are sitting in your house inside the fort, waiting for the **scribe** to arrive to write down your invitation. This scribe writes your husband's letters for him. He comes often because your husband writes to many soldiers in the forts in the north. Sometimes he writes to soldiers stationed in London.

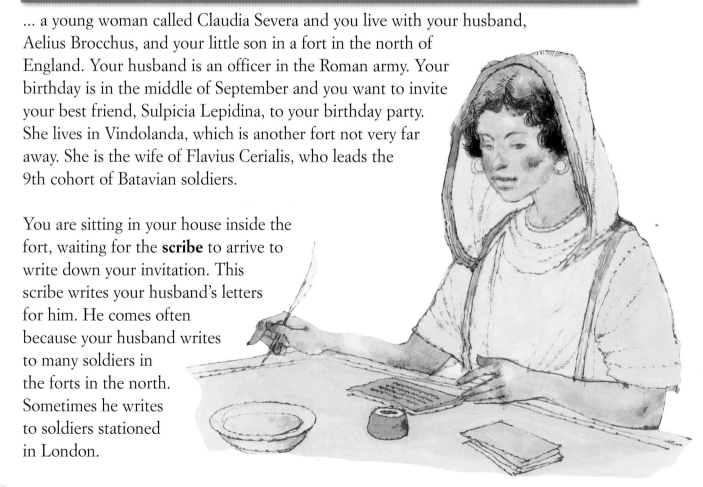

Here is the scribe! He sits down on a stool near you and brings out a thin wooden tablet from his leather bag. Then he takes out an inkwell and a reed pen and asks what you want to say. You've planned it in your mind already so you can tell him immediately what to write …

A Roman inkwell with the name of the owner, Iucundus, scratched on it.

'Claudia Severa to her Lepidina greetings. On the third day before the Ides of September, sister, for the day of the celebration of my birthday, I give you a warm invitation to make sure that you come to us, to make the day more enjoyable for me by your arrival if you are present. Give my greetings to your Cerialis. My Aelius and my little son send him their greetings.'

This is what is left of the actual birthday invitation, written on wooden tablets for Claudia Severa about AD 100. It was found at Vindolanda in 1985.

Has he got all of that down? He writes very quickly, dipping his pen into the inkwell now and again. He writes a column down one side of the tablet and then he goes on to a second column on the same side. He hasn't made any mistakes.

Now it's your turn. You want to sign off the letter. He dips the reed pen in the inkwell and hands it to you. You write: *'Farewell, sister, my dearest soul, as I hope to prosper, and hail.'* You hand the tablet back to the scribe. He folds it down the middle between the columns of writing and, on the back on the right half, he writes:
'To Sulpicia Lepidina, wife of Cerialis, from Severa.'

He puts the tablet in his bag. He'll give it to the soldier who is riding off this very morning to Vindolanda with other letters. He carries letters twice a week between the two forts. You are impatient to have a reply from Sulpicia. Will she be able to come to your birthday party? Maybe the soldier will bring back her answer!

The letter on page 23 is one of the earliest examples we have of Latin written by a woman. Claudia Severa would either have gone to a school for boys and girls until she was about twelve, or she would have been taught how to write at home, perhaps by an educated slave. Although she wrote part of this letter herself, the **scribe,** or secretary, wrote most of it for her. He also wrote official and private letters for her husband, Flavius Cerialis.

THE VINDOLANDA TABLETS

Hundreds of parts of wooden writing tablets have been dug up by **archaeologists** at Vindolanda, which is near Hadrian's Wall in the north of England. Luckily the tablets have lasted down through the centuries. They tell us a lot about how the Romans lived when they conquered Britain and also about how they wrote.

Most of the tablets were originally about the size of a postcard. They were sometimes strung together like this.

Some of the tablets are military documents. Some are letters that were sent to, or written by, the soldiers who were stationed there. They are written in Latin. This was the language used by the Romans throughout the countries that they conquered and that became part of the Roman empire. We can tell from the number of letters that quite a few soldiers could write, even if they sometimes used a scribe, or a secretary, to write for them.

THE ROMAN ALPHABET

The Romans used an alphabet they may have borrowed from the Greeks or it may have come from the Etruscans, who lived in the centre of what is modern Italy. The Etruscans used early Greek letters but they also had their own signs. The Romans changed the letters slightly to suit their language. Gradually all the countries in the Roman empire began to use the Roman alphabet and the Roman language, Latin.

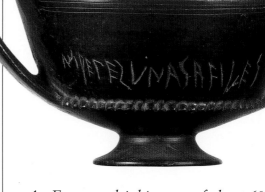

An Etruscan drinking cup of about 600 BC. The Etruscan writing runs from right to left. It says 'I belong to Avile Repesuna'.

The Roman alphabet.

A military diploma written on bronze plates. It was issued in AD 103 by the emperor Trajan to Reburrus, a Spanish officer who had completed his service in the army. The emperor grants him Roman citizenship and the right to marry.

The Romans wrote with pen and ink on wooden tablets or papyrus (like the Egyptians), or they used a **stylus** to write on wooden tablets covered with wax. Roman authors, such as Virgil and Horace and Cicero and Ovid, wrote on papyrus.

When there was a victory to celebrate, such as the defeat of an enemy army, or they wanted to praise a great emperor, the Romans would build huge monuments.

A Roman wooden writing tablet and styli (the plural of 'stylus'). The tablet was covered with wax and the writer pressed the stylus into the wax to write.

As a first step, the stone mason would draw some guidelines on the stone with chalk, then he would paint the letters, fitting the top and bottom of each letter between the guidelines. After that he would use a chisel to carve out the inscription. If you look carefully you will see that the lines are sometimes thick and sometimes thin.

A wall painting from the Roman city of Pompeii. The man holds a book scroll and the woman holds a stylus and a writing tablet.

Part of a Roman imperial inscription.

Roman monuments often had written inscriptions, so people could read who put up the monument, and why. The writing was in capital letters. Some of the letters have a little line, called a 'serif', used as a finishing stroke. The letters of the type in this book also use serifs. Can you see them?

Serif AVE

5 Monks and manuscripts

'If you do not know what writing is, you may think it is not specially difficult … Let me tell you that it is an arduous task: it destroys your eyesight, bends your spine, squeezes your stomach and your sides, and makes your whole body ache.'

In the Middle Ages monks made copies of religious books. They wrote 'manuscripts', which is the Latin word for 'written by hand'. These sentences were written by the monk who copied a manuscript called a *Beatus* in a Spanish monastery in the 12th century. At the end of the manuscript he complained how hard the work was in a **colophon**.

You are …

… a **novice**. You have just joined a group of monks living in a monastery, and one day, when you are older, you will become a monk like them. In these first few months you have been told to help one of the monks and learn from him how to write. His name is Brother John. You are sitting with him and twenty other monks in a large room. It is called the *scriptorium*, which is Latin for 'writing room'. The monks are making copies of old religious books to put in the library. Brother John can read them.

You are just learning how to read. Brother John is teaching you.

Apart from getting up every four hours to say prayers, you have been sitting there for the whole day. It is cold and you aren't allowed to light candles in here because you might start a fire. When it gets too dark to see properly you will stop work. Nobody talks.

The monk on the left is sharpening his quill. The other monk is scraping parchment.

When you first arrived, Brother John showed you how to prepare the sheets of parchment he is writing on. Parchment is made from the skins of calves. He showed you how to take a calf skin from a lime bath, where it had been soaking, and scrub it so that there was no hair left on it. Then you had to stretch it out on a wooden frame to dry. Next you scraped it again to make sure it was smooth but, even so, Brother John smoothed it again with his knife before he started writing on it. You didn't like that job. The parchment smells horrible when it's wet – and not much better when it's dry.

Then Brother John showed you how to cut the quills he uses for writing. They are made from big goose feathers. You cut the end to make it sharp and then make a slit in the middle of the sharp end. Brother John uses a knife to shape each quill just how he wants it. He has to keep on sharpening it while he's writing because it gets worn down quite quickly.

Drawing guidelines on the parchment.

The best job is drawing lines on the parchment. Brother John has given you a ruler and shown you how to draw lines to guide him when he writes. You have to hold the parchment on a board and rest it on your knees. It's very difficult to draw straight lines that way. You're doing that now and your back hurts and your fingers are cold and stiff.

He's promised that one day he will let you do some copying from a book! Just the easy copying: no capital letters and certainly none of those tiny pictures of animals and flowers and people.

Even Brother John makes mistakes sometimes with his copying. Another monk looks at what he's written and corrects it if a letter or word has been left out or wrongly spelled. If it's only one letter, Brother John scrapes it out with his knife and writes in the correct one. But if he's left out a few words, he writes them in the margin and draws an arrow to show where they should go.

Oh how your back hurts now. The light has almost gone. Surely it's time to stop. You can hardly see to draw the lines. Yes! At last Brother John is standing up and stretching and rubbing his hands. Time to go!

A page from a Bible, produced in the scriptorium at Winchester Priory in the 12th century AD. You can see that a monk has pointed out mistakes in the copying (on the right).

In the Middle Ages very few people could read or write. Even the great emperor Charlemagne, who ruled over most of Europe, signed all his royal documents with a cross because he couldn't write his own name. Only the monks knew enough to make copies of religious books. They kept them in their libraries or made them for rich people to have in their homes, even if they could not read them. Just making a single book by hand could take several days of hard work, or a lot longer in some cases, so not many were produced.

The emperor Charlemagne.

DECORATION

The monks did not just copy the writing. Some of them, called illuminators, decorated the pages with little pictures of birds, animals, people and flowers. The initial letters of paragraphs and chapters were all decorated as well. Sometimes they used gold leaf, which made the pictures even more beautiful.

Charlemagne loved books although he couldn't read. He invited an English scholar called Alcuin to come to France to teach **scribes** new ways of handwriting. French monks were using the Roman alphabet in the 8th century AD. Alcuin worked out a system for dividing their writing into sentences and paragraphs, like we do today, so that now the initial letters at the beginning of paragraphs were very important and were decorated to make them stand out on the page.

A page from a prayer book called 'The Hours of Elizabeth the Queen' (1420). The picture shows the Last Supper. The writing is Psalm 94.

PARCHMENT

Parchment was much easier to use than papyrus had been. It was possible to fold the sheets of parchment and stitch them together to make a book.

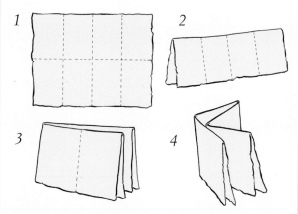

Once the sheets were all stitched together, the bookbinder made a cover out of wood covered in leather.

THE DEMAND FOR BOOKS

Gradually more people began to learn to read and write. Books were in great demand – not only religious books, but also books about medicine, law, mathematics and astronomy. And by the end of the 12th century AD the writing was not always in Latin. Now books could be found written in English, French or Italian. Scribes who were not monks, but who worked together in workshops, copied books for more and more people. There was almost too much work for them to do. Copying, decorating and binding each book took a long time.

Christine de Pisan lived in France in the 14th century. She wrote several books about famous women.

Part of a page from the Luttrell Psalter (AD 1340). The scribe has copied out Psalm 95 and an artist has decorated the page with pictures of people harvesting.

6 The invention of printing

This is the **colophon** at the end of a Bible. It explains that the book was not written with 'the scratchings of a pen'. It was made by 'the artificial printing of letters' in 1462. The two printers have signed their names, Johannes Fust and Peter Schoiffer. They have put their **device** at the bottom. Their printing workshop probably had the same device, or sign, hanging above the door.

You are ...

... an apprentice, training to become a printer. You have only been in the workshop for a few weeks and the first job you've been given to do isn't very difficult. You have to stand at a table in front of the printing press and lay the sheets of paper, which have been printed flat, on the table. Then, after you've gathered a few sheets together, you hang them up on the line, like washing, so that the ink and the paper can dry. It's not very exciting, but if you do this job well perhaps the master printer who owns the workshop will give you something more interesting to do.

The man sitting next to you has a pile of different letters and numbers made of metal. He is putting them into a wooden case, called a type case. The case is divided up into different-sized squares and he's sorting the letters into the squares in a special order. The letters of the alphabet that are used most often (such as e, i, h

A printer's workshop. On the far left are the compositors. To the right of them a man is putting letters into a type case. The master printer stands on the right.

and o) are in the centre in the large squares, and the ones that are not used very much (such as z, x, j and w) are in the outside squares.

The men sitting a bit further away from you are called 'compositors'. Each compositor has sheets of handwriting stuck up on the wall in front of him and a type case on the

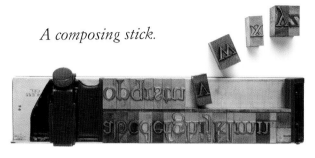

A composing stick.

table. They pick out the metal letters they need to make up the words written on the paper. It's easier for them if all the most frequently used letters are where they can quickly reach them. They put the letters into a 'stick' that holds them together in a line. They also put little pieces of lead between the words to make the spaces. They work very quickly and soon they have lots of lines of finished print.

Each line of print goes on to a kind of metal table, one under the other. When they have 'composed' enough lines to fill a page, with pieces of lead where there are to be blank spaces on the printed page, they start on the next page. For the book they are working on now they will need to make up eight pages of metal letters to fit into the 'forme', which will go into the press to be printed on one sheet of paper.

One job you might be given soon is to ink the type when it's in the forme. To do this you will have to use two ink balls. You rub the metal letters with them so that they are covered in ink. The little pieces of lead between the words are lower than the letters, so they don't pick up any of the ink. Then, when the forme is all inked, a sheet of damp paper is put on a frame. The frame is folded down on to the forme and pushed in, under the press. Then two press men turn a handle that makes the press squeeze the paper down on to the forme. When they take paper out it is printed with the letters (now the right way around) that are on the forme.

You will have to learn to all those different jobs while you are an apprentice. It takes a long time and you will stay in this workshop for seven years. You're called the 'printer's devil' by the men, but you don't mind that. Once you have served your apprenticeship you can become what is called a 'journeyman'. This means that you can go out and work in other printing workshops. Then, one day, you might become a master printer. You'd better start hanging up some of those sheets of printed paper otherwise the master will soon be after you!

The Chinese had invented printing by the 11th century AD. They used letters made from clay and glue rather than metal. By the 15th century, the Koreans were making letters out of bronze. In Europe the first time anybody wrote about printing was in 1471. A man called Gasparino Barzizza wrote: 'There was near Mainz [in Germany] a certain Johann surnamed Gutenberg, who was the very first man to devise the art of printing by which books were not written, as they used to be, with … a pen … but by metal characters.' Gutenberg had realized that letters, or

Johannes Gutenberg

'type', could be made of metal. The letters could be made up into words, then taken apart and used to make different words on another page when the first was printed.

MOVEABLE TYPE

Between 1452 and 1455 Gutenberg produced the first book to be printed using moveable type. This book was a Bible, now known as the Gutenberg Bible (pictured below). You can see that it looks like the manuscripts that the monks wrote and illuminated (see pages 27–31). Only the small letters have been printed. An illuminator has added the initial letters and all the decorations by hand once the pages were printed.

Gutenberg probably did not print anything else because his printing business was not very successful and he ran out of money. But in 1457 another man called Peter Schoeffer printed a book of prayers called a Psalter. This time, everything on the pages was printed. The 'type' was made of a mixture of lead, tin and antimony.

A page from 'The Canterbury Tales'.

in Germany but he was working in Bruges, in Belgium, when he printed the first book in English. It was a book originally written in French that Caxton had translated into English. The name of the book was *The Recuyell of the Histories of Troy*.

PRINTING COMES TO ENGLAND

Soon there were printing workshops opening throughout Europe. The first English printer was a man called William Caxton. He probably learned how to print

Caxton went back to England and set up a printing press in London. One of the most famous books he printed there was *The Canterbury Tales* by Geoffrey Chaucer, which was written in the 14th century.

PAPER-MAKING

As well as being the first people to develop print, the Chinese were also the first to make paper. They started making paper out of rags in 104 AD, but it was not until 1488 that the first papermill opened in England. Before that date, all the paper used had to be imported.

To make paper, rags were shredded and put into a great tub of water until the fibres separated. The papermaker then dipped a wire frame into the mixture and when it came out there was a thin layer of fibres covering the frame. The wire frame then had to be pressed to remove all the water before being hung up to dry. In the picture of the workshop on page 32 a boy is coming through the door with sheets of paper from the papermaker.

People began to use paper instead of parchment for writing by hand as well as for printing. Paper was cheaper to buy and much easier to use.

7 Beautiful writing

what Advances I have made in my Writing. I find now by Experience, that to write a bold free hand correctly, requires no Small Care and Application

'I find now by experience that to write a bold free hand correctly requires no small care and application.'

This sentence is part of a letter written by a boy to his father in 1774. It is used as a good example of letter writing in a teaching book called *Webb's Useful Penmanship*, written in 1796. It was important for boys to learn how to write well so that they could write business letters and lists of figures when they took their first jobs.

You are ...

... nine years old. You live in a big house in the country and you are sitting at a table in the library waiting for your writing master to arrive to give you a lesson. Because you are a girl you have all your lessons at home. Your brother, who is one year older than you, has gone away to boarding school. He is learning to write, and now and again he sends you a letter. You send him letters back to show him that you can write just as well as he can.

Sometimes you write a message to your friend Priscilla, who lives in the town 8 km (5 miles) away.

On the table in front of you, you have your inkwell, your quill pen and a pouncepot filled with chalk powder to dry the ink. You also have some sheets of white paper to write on. This time you are not going to drop great ink blots all over the sheet, like you did last lesson! Here comes Mr Prentice. 'Ah! I see you are all ready for me. That is excellent. I have brought you a new book to look at,' he says.

He shows the book to you. 'This contains information about the Italian hand that you have been learning. I particularly want you to observe the manner of holding your quill, which is so well illustrated on this page,' he says. 'You are sometimes a trifle amiss in that respect.'

Oh dear! You know you are, but it is uncomfortable holding the quill in the correct position for more than a few words.

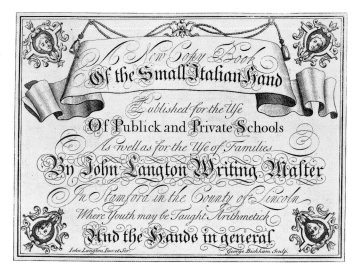

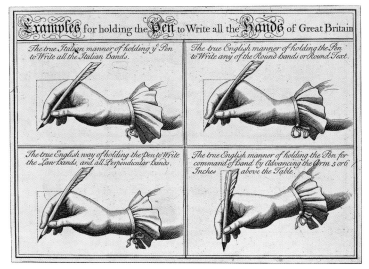

He turns his attention to the page. 'Now, show me how you hold your quill for the Italian hand.' You pick up the quill and try to copy the position of the fingers and thumb from the picture in front of you. 'That is definitely better,' he says. 'Take some ink and we shall try to copy this sentence, paying due attention to the position of the quill. Have you sharpened it?' Of course you have! You spent your time waiting for him sharpening the point.

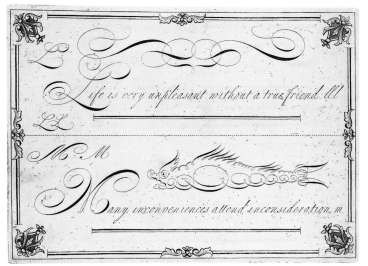

A page from the 18th-century book, Of the Small Italian Hand.

You start copying, trying hard not to make any blots, to hold the quill correctly and to spell the words. You like writing. Your father has promised that if you write a letter to your brother he will send one of the servants to ride into town this afternoon with it, along with one of his own letters. The servant will give your letter to the mail coach to deliver to the school. As soon as the lesson is over you will start your brother's letter.

As more and more books were printed, so more and more people learned to read and write. During the 16th, 17th and 18th centuries writing masters wrote copy books. These demonstrated how to write using different, and sometimes very complicated, styles.

A copybook, published in 1618.

As well as copying the handwriting, you were also meant to think about the words that you were copying. They were mostly about good behaviour!

SIMPLIFIED HANDWRITING

Calligraphy, which means 'beautiful writing', was considered to be an important skill for young girls as well as boys to learn. But by the 18th century all the elaborate curls and squiggles that were part of the earlier styles were too difficult and too slow to produce if you were writing every day for your work. Boys were being taught a simple style called 'copperplate' and the 'Italian hand' was thought to be very suitable for 'ladies', since the letters were small and clear.

> *Mrs. Temple begs to announce, that in addition to her Wax Flowers in the Great Exhibition, (Number 61. Class 29,) she has an extensive Collection of Native and Tropical Flowers at the Bazaar and her Private Residence; the whole of the Flowers and Foliage modelled by herself from nature.*

'Copperplate'.

The 'Italian hand'.

Gradually, as more and more schools were opened, it was not only the children of rich families who were educated and learned how to read and write. In the 19th century boys and girls spent some part of every day sitting at their wooden desks carefully copying out sentences like this.

> *Ottawa possesses rich pine forests. O*

> *Pumas is a native of tropical America*

An Edwardian classroom.

NEW WRITING TOOLS

Instead of using quill pens, which you had to sharpen all the time, people started to use pens made of horn and tortoiseshell. These pens were much harder and so lasted longer. Then a pen was invented with a wooden handle and a steel nib that you could change if it wore out. But although this type of pen was much better than using a quill, you still had to keep dipping the nib into an inkwell to fill it with ink. It was very easy to make blots

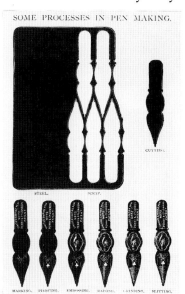

on your page, especially if you accidentally overfilled your nib with ink. You needed to have blotting paper at hand to soak up the ink.

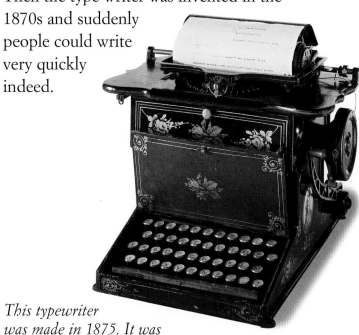

A fountain pen, made in the US about a hundred years ago.

The next invention to make handwriting easier was the fountain pen. Ink was held inside the pen so that you did not have to keep dipping the nib into an inkwell. You had to fill the pen with ink when you had used it all up. Now we use pens that don't need filling with ink at all.

An early ballpoint pen from 1945. We often call these pens 'biros' after the man who invented them, Laszlo Jozsef Biro.

Then the type writer was invented in the 1870s and suddenly people could write very quickly indeed.

This typewriter was made in 1875. It was invented in the US by Christopher Latham Stoles and Samuel Soule. The keys are arranged in the same order (QWERTY ... etc) that we use on computer keyboards today.

8 Chinese characters

'Sincerity makes for correct brushwork.'

This was written in the 9th century AD by by a famous Chinese calligrapher called Liu Gongquan. Calligraphy is the art of beautiful, decorative writing. In the past, Chinese people considered that only good, moral people could create fine writing. Chinese **script** is one of the oldest kinds of writing in the world still used by people today.

You are ...

... sitting at your desk in the classroom. Sitting next to you is your friend Ma Yong. You are watching the teacher write a **character** on the blackboard. 'You remember that this character means "animal"?' Yes, you remember it well. You had to copy it fifty times for homework last week. 'Now, can you tell me what this means?' The teacher puts another character on the board after the animal character. Hands go up in the air. Everybody tries hard to answer. Li Hua thinks she knows what is it. 'A fox?' 'That's it,' says the teacher. 'Good girl! The fox is a cunning animal. He plays tricks on other animals, so this word can also mean "cunning". Will you remember that? Now we're going to learn how to write it. Have you all got your exercise books ready?'

animal

fox

You open your book and find a clean page. The page is divided into squares. You pick up your biro and start to follow the teacher's instructions.

A Chinese silk scroll from the 19th century. Words and pictures together create a harmonious image.

'First we'll write "animal". Remember we start with the first stroke in the top left hand square. You write a short stroke going down from right to left. Then the second stroke runs across the first stroke down from the left into the bottom square and turns up at the bottom. Then the third stroke runs down from the second stroke to the left and just a little way into the bottom square.'

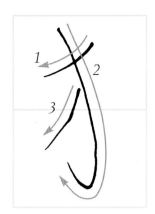

That's easy. You know where the strokes go. But here comes the new bit. 'We start in the top square on your page. First there's the stroke down from right to left. Then there's the second stroke joining the first and going down into the bottom square. Then there's the third stroke down into the bottom square and going up at the end. The fourth stroke is just the little squiggle at the end of the third stroke. The fifth stroke is another one going down into the bottom square. Now you've written fox!'

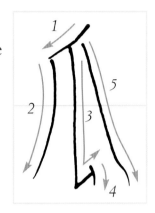

You try hard to copy exactly what she has written on the board and to keep the strokes inside the squares. She'll be showing you how to write another nine new characters during this lesson, and then you will have to take your book home after school and copy them all out over and over again until you can write them neatly and remember what they mean.

A Chinese calligraphy brush, paper, ink and ink stone.

The lesson you really like happens only once a week. It is the calligraphy lesson. You learn how to write all those characters the way the ancient **scribes** used to. Instead of a biro, you use a brush made of different animal hairs, such as goat and rabbit. You have an ink stone and an ink stick, which is made from charcoal and animal glue. You pour some water on to the stone and grind the ink stick into the puddle until it turns into black ink. Sometimes you just take an ink bottle into the class with the charcoal already mixed in the water. You use your brush to write the strokes. The squares on your paper are much bigger and the paper is thicker than in your exercise book. You try to write the characters as beautifully as you can. One day you want your writing to be good enough to be hung up on the classroom wall.

The children in the class on pages 40-41 are learning how to write a script that has not changed very much over the last 3,000 years. The **characters** do not stand for letters of an alphabet, like ours do: they stand for sounds, like 'ba', 'ma', 'ban', or 'chong'. A few characters, which could be the oldest in the language, still clearly stand for things or ideas.

Early picture sign	*Zhou or Qin Dynasty*	*Han Dynasty 206BC - AD220*	*Standard sign*
rain			
water			
fish			

In the West, children have to learn an alphabet of twenty-six letters. Chinese children have to learn 2,500 characters by the time they are eleven years old.

ORACLE BONES

The earliest Chinese writing, which was found by **archaeologists** in the 19th century, was on bits of cows' shoulder blades and on turtle shells. Thousands of these bits of bone with marks on them were found at a place called Anyang, not far north of the Yellow River. The ancient kings of a people who called themselves the Shang wanted to know what the gods thought was going to happen in the future. Their **soothsayers** heated the bones in a fire until they cracked. According to which way the cracks ran, the soothsayers scratched the kings' questions and gods' answers on to the bones. The writing on these 'oracle bones' was like this.

From that time 3,000 years ago, the number of characters has grown and grown to more than 40,000. Nowadays people need to know about 3,000 characters to be able to read a newspaper. They can sometimes guess what a character means from the way it looks and sometimes they can guess from using the characters they already know (like 'tree').

木　　林　　森

tree　　*wood*　　*forest*

CALLIGRAPHY

In calligraphy lessons, Chinese children are taught to try to make their writing as beautiful as if they were painting a picture. They try to copy the greatest achievements in writing from hundreds of years ago. Here is the writing of Wang Xizhi, one of the greatest writers and judges of writing, who lived in the 3rd century AD.

Wang Xizhi followed strict rules about the order in which the strokes that make up a character should be written. The strokes going across – the horizontal lines – are always written before the strokes going down – the vertical lines. You can see how this works in the word 'fox' on page 41.

Chinese children today have to learn all the same rules.

合九玉石落、是吾寶子
之何不守心曉根帶養華
天順地合藏精七日之奇
相舍崑崙之性不迷誤九

9 What next?

Now we can communicate with other people in a few seconds by using a computer. We can send messages to our friends all over the world, as though we were talking to them, we can chat to them in chat rooms, or we can write long essays and books. Those have to be written much more carefully.

cn U cum 2 a pRT?

Today lots of us use mobile phones to send text messages to our friends. Is texting creating a whole new written language?

We don't always have to use our hands to write. Special computer programs mean that you can just talk and the computer will write the words on the screen.

We can find out information from the internet and we can even read books on the internet. We can publish our own newspapers and books. We can decide how we want the writing to look by choosing which font to use and how the page should be laid out.

A school newspaper, created on a computer that allows the writers to choose different fonts (styles of type).

In many (but not all) countries in the world children go to school to learn how to read and write and how to use computers. We don't need **scribes** any more because we can write for ourselves. What we write can be sent to the reader very quickly even if he or she lives thousands of miles away.

In the West we are still using what was originally the Roman alphabet and we still use **pictograms** and **ideograms**.

In other parts of the world different scripts are used – you can see some examples on the next page. Do you think in the future we shall all use the same script? What do you think might happen in the next few years to the way we write things down?

10 A world of writing

Today, people all over the world use many different scripts in many different languages. Here are some of them.

The Cyrillic alphabet is used to write the Russian language.

«Люди в разных странах мира используют разные виды письма для разных языков. Это образец письма на русском языке с применением кириллицы, используемый в России».

This devanagari script is used in India to write the modern language Hindi.

दुनिया के अलग अलग देशों की भाषाएँ अलग अलग लिपियों में लिखी जाती हैं । यह नमूना दवनागरी लिपि में है ; इस लिपि का प्रयोग हिन्दी के लिए किया जाता है, जो भारत में बोली जाती है ।

The Hebrew script, used in Israel.

אנשים בכל רחבי העולם משתמשים בהרבה סוגי כתב שונים בהרבה שפות שונות. דוגמת כתב זו היא בעברית, המדוברת בישראל.

These Japanese sentences are written in the kanji and hiragana scripts. Kanji was originally based on Chinese characters.

世界中の人々は多くの異なる言語で、それぞれ異なる文字を使っています。 この文書の見本は（ひらがな、漢字）が使用され、（日本）で使われています。

Korean script.

"전세계에서는 다양한 언어와 문자가 쓰여지고 있습니다. 이 글은 한반도에서 쓰이는 한국어의 문자 체계인 한글로 쓰여졌습니다."

الشُّعوب في جَميع أنحَاء العَالَم يستَعمِلون مَخطوطَاتٍ في لُغَاتٍ مُتعَدِّدة . هذِه العَينة المُدَوَّنة هي مِنَ الخَطِّ النَّسخي المُتَداوَل في كَافة الدُّول والشُّعوب العَربيَّة .

The naskhi script is widely used all over the Arab world.

Glossary

Archaeologist A person who looks at the remains of the past – for example, ancient buildings, tombs, or pottery – to find out more about how people lived at that time.

Character A sign used in a writing system or script.

Colophon A piece of writing placed at the end of a book giving information about its publication. It can be just the publisher's trademark.

Consonant A letter of the alphabet that is used with vowels to make a word (see also vowel). You use your lips or your tongue to make the sound of a consonant. In the English alphabet the consonants are: b, c, d, f, g, h, j, k, l, m, n, p, q, r, s, t, v, w, x, y, z.

Decipher To work out how to read something that is difficult to understand, such as a code or an unknown writing system.

Demotic script The everyday writing used by the ancient Egyptian people after the 7th century BC.

Determinative An Egyptian hieroglyphic sign that explains what kind of word you are reading. It has no sound. It is always placed at the end of a word.

Device A sign, rather like a coat of arms, that is used like a badge by one person or a family.

Hieratic A type of hieroglyphs used by the priests of ancient Egypt.

Ideogram A sign that stands for an idea or an object without telling you how it should sound. For example, in English we use the sign & to stand for 'and', or the sign @ for 'at'.

Logogram A single symbol that stands for a whole word or phrase. For example, the symbol % stands for 'per cent'.

Novice A person who is new or inexperienced, such as a trainee monk.

Oracle A prediction made by a holy person about what is going to happen in the future.

Phonogram A sign that stands for a sound. In English, for example, the phonogram 'l' stands for the sound at the beginning of the word 'leaf'.

Pictogram A sign that looks like a picture of an object.

Scholar A person who studies a subject in great detail and is very knowledgeable.

Scribe In history, someone who knows how to write. Scribes wrote down what people said, or copied writing.

Script Any particular type of writing.

Soothsayer A person who claims to be able to tell what is going to happen in the future.

Stylus A sharp, pointed piece of wood, or other material, used for writing.

Syllable A group of letters or sounds including one vowel. When syllables are put together they can make a word. For example, in the word 'teacher' there are two syllables: 'teach' and 'er'.

Vowel In the English alphabet the vowels are: a, e, i, o, u. They are used on their own or with other vowels and with a consonant or a group of consonants to make a word. Vowel sounds are made in your throat without using your tongue.

Map

A map of the world showing where the different kinds of writing in this book, both ancient and modern, come from.

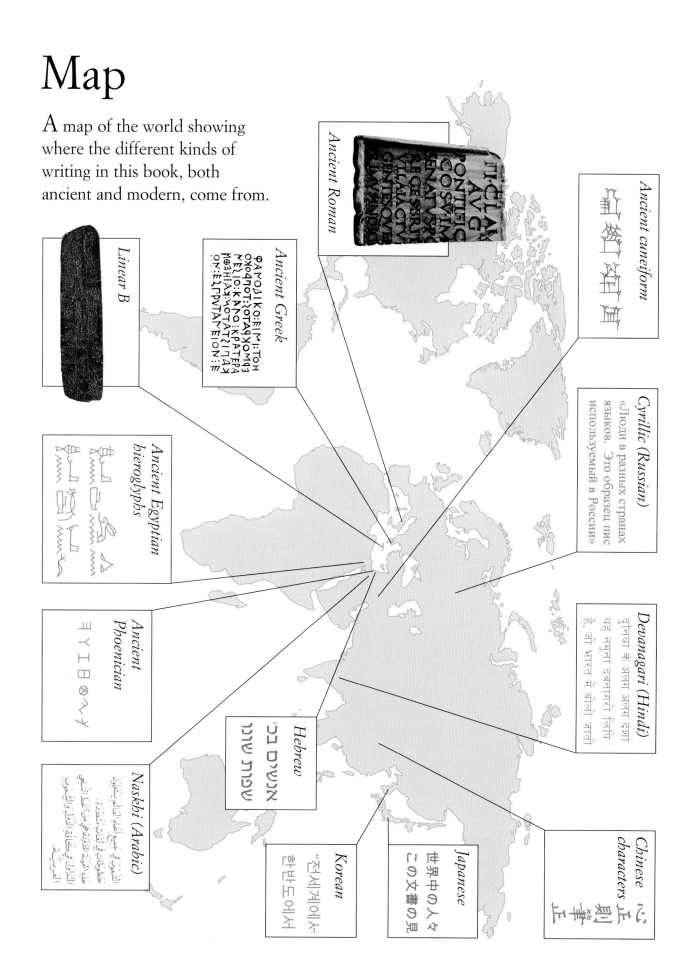

Ancient Roman

Ancient cuneiform

Linear B

Ancient Greek
ΦΑΛΟΟΙΚΟ:ΕΙΜΙ:ΤΟΝ
ΟΚΟΟΝΟΤ:ΧΟΤΑΧΧΟΜΟΟ
ΜΕΓΙΟ:ΚΑΛΟ:ΚΡΑΤΕΡΑ
ΜΘΕΙΗΙΑΧΜΟΤΑΤΖΊΓΠΑΣ
ΟΝ:ΕΙΓΡΥΤΑΜΕΙΟΝ:Ε

Cyrillic (Russian)
«Люди в разных странах
языков. Это образец пис
используемый в России»

Ancient Egyptian
hieroglyphs

Devanagari (Hindi)
दुनिया के अलग अलग देशों
यह नमूना देवनागरी लिपि
है, जो भारत में बोली जाती

Ancient
Phoenician
ヨＹＩＯ⊗~ㄨ

Hebrew
אנשים שונים
שפות שונות
זהו דוגמה

Naskhi (Arabic)

Korean
"전세계에서
한반도에서

Japanese
世界中の人々
この文書の見

Chinese
characters
心 正
則 書
正

MAP 47

Index

Further reading

FOR CHILDREN

The Mystery of the Hieroglyphs, Carol Donoughue, BMP 1999
Pocket Guide to Ancient Egyptian Hieroglyphs, Richard Parkinson, BMP 2003
The British Museum Illustrated Encyclopaedia of Ancient Egypt, Geraldine Harris and Delia Pemberton, BMP 2005 (second edition, with links to British Museum websites)
The British Museum Illustrated Encyclopaedia of Ancient Greece, Sean Sheehan, BMP 2002
The British Museum Illustrated Encyclopaedia of Ancient Rome, Mike Corbishley, BMP 2003

FOR ADULTS

Scribes, Script and Books, Leila Avrin, British Library/American Library Association, 1991
The Story of Writing: alphabets, hieroglyphs and pictograms, Andrew Robinson, Thames and Hudson, 2000
Writing: the story of alphabets and scripts, Georges Jean, Thames and Hudson, 1992

WEBSITES FOR CHILDREN AND ADULTS

The British Library: www.bl.uk
The British Museum: www.thebritishmuseum.ac.uk for online information about objects, tours and games.
An online edition of the Roman writing tablets found at Vindolanda (see Chapter 4):
http:// vindolanda.csad.ox.ac.uk